Self-Care
Rules

Self-Care Rules

100 WAYS TO TEND TO YOUR BODY, MIND, AND SPIRIT

Sumathi Reddy

UNION
SQUARE
& CO.

NEW YORK

**UNION
SQUARE
& CO.**

NEW YORK

UNION SQUARE & CO. and the distinctive Union Square & Co. logo are
trademarks of Sterling Publishing Co., Inc.

Union Square & Co., LLC, is a subsidiary of Sterling Publishing Co., Inc.

ISBN 978-1-4549-5247-3
ISBN 978-1-4549-5248-0 (e-book)

Library of Congress Control Number: 2024935085

For information about custom editions, special sales, and premium purchases,
please contact specialsales@unionsquareandco.com.

Printed in China

2 4 6 8 10 9 7 5 3 1

unionsquareandco.com

Cover and interior design by Renée Bollier
Cover and interior illustrations by Olivia Herrick

For all the moms out there who take care of so many others and often don't find time for themselves.

This is for you.

Contents

INTRODUCTION

It took a pandemic for me to discover self-care.

Despite being a consumer health columnist at the *Wall Street Journal* for nearly a decade, my definition of self-care had been eating a lousy salad for lunch and dragging myself to a spin class that felt like bodily torture. Or maybe getting a massage when I had a spare hour in between work, soccer carpools, and PTA meetings.

When Covid-19 shut the world down, things abruptly changed for me. At first, for the worse. But then with more time, fewer obligations, and boredom, things changed. I went on weekly weekend hikes with my children. I took daily walks with my neighbor, discovering new streets and pocket parks in the neighborhood I'd been living in for more than a decade. I taught my six-year-old to ride a bike, and we went on bike rides during my lunch break. I enrolled in a tennis class—a sport I had never played—and outdoor exercise classes I actually enjoyed. I learned to make homemade pizza and salads that were surprisingly delicious. I enrolled in an improv class and laughed harder than I have in ages. I even got a full night's sleep.

I discovered what self-care was for me. As a result I was a better mother, spouse, daughter, friend, and even reporter—I was logging more hours than ever working and covering the Covid-19 pandemic as a health columnist.

We are constantly taking care of others. Yes, in this whirlwind juggle it's very easy to forget the most important person: ourselves. Self-care often falls by the wayside. Yet we forget an important truth: we can't take care of others if we don't take care of ourselves.

I have found the key to self-care is making it a ritual, a habit, something you do again and again. Incorporate different forms of self-care into your daily or weekly routine. Taking incremental steps can lead to fulfilling larger goals: For example, my tennis lessons have turned into regular doubles games with people whose company I enjoy. This is exercise and socialization that I look forward to. It's OK if you miss a day or even a week of something. Perhaps the greatest form of self-care is having patience with yourself and forgiving yourself when you don't meet your goals.

In researching this book, I found most evidence-based self-care tips seemed to fall into one of three categories: things that nurture the mind, the body, or the spirit.

Our physical health is the form of self-care that we typically think of. Eating a healthy diet, getting some form of physical activity regularly, and getting enough and quality sleep are among the most important pillars of physical health. But there are many other ways of taking care of our bodies, from getting regular checkups to wearing sunscreen and giving our eyes a break from digital strain.

Our mental and emotional health directly impacts our physical health. Setting boundaries with people at work and home, staying connected with friends and families and even acquaintances, and seeking adventure, laughter, and new experiences all help promote our mental and emotional health.

Finally, nurturing our spiritual self is also an important part of self-care. Meditating or even the act of breathing helps us connect with ourselves. Taking a break, be it from social media or work or just pausing to surrender to silence or nature are all important ways to reset. Having a gratitude practice, volunteering, or paying it forward with random acts of kindness help strengthen our spirit.

An important thing to consider is balancing the different forms of self-care. You can exercise every day, but it's just as important to cultivate emotional and mental forms of self-care. So if you work out every day, try skipping one and use that time to get a coffee with a friend. Or better yet, go on a walk outdoors with a friend during your lunch break and eat outside. You're getting fresh air, socialization, exercise, and a mental break. Four forms of self-care in one act!

Consider this a book you can turn to when you're in need of inspiration. You can read it cover to cover or feel free to open it to any page when you need a simple tip or two or guidance to improve some aspect of your life. I know from the research—and my own experience—that those changes to your daily rhythms and routines can lead to larger, positive changes in your life.

PART ONE

Body

Mind

Spirit

Include Sleep in Your Diet

Binging on popcorn in the evening? Try getting more sleep. Studies show getting your z's—seven to nine hours per night—could help you eat in moderation. You're also less likely to fill up on salty, fatty, and sugary foods as quick fuel.

Curb the Midnight Munchies

The clock is inching toward midnight, and all of a sudden you're having cravings for potato chips or popcorn. Try to avoid snacking or eating after dinner or dessert. Late-night snacks tend to be processed foods or foods high in sugar and fat. Because your metabolism slows down at night, the calories are often stored as fat. Late-night eating can also interfere with sleep. If your body is still digesting food, lying down and going to sleep may result in digestive problems, such as heartburn.

The Sound of Sleep

Get a sound machine, particularly if you live in a noisy environment or get woken up easily. Use an app to figure out which frequency works best for you.

- White noise is the most well-known of frequencies and uses a mix of sound frequencies resulting in a static-like sound. It's good at masking other loud noises, and studies have found it can improve sleep. It's commonly used with babies.

- Pink noise consists of deeper and lower sound waves and may be more soothing than white noise. It has a consistent pitch for a steady sound.

- Brown noise, which is lower in frequencies, is a bit rougher with a deep and steady sound.

4

Actually Rest on Your Sick Day

It seems obvious: stay home from work when you're sick. But the culture of working through sickness pervades, and so many of us martyr our way into the office when we're feeling down. This serves no one. First, you are possibly infecting your colleagues with your germs. And when it comes to your own self-care, resting will help speed up your own recovery. Try to avoid working from home, especially if you're running a fever. It's OK to respond to emails if you're up for it, but take a nap and truly rest so you're fully recovered when you return to work.

Skip the Chips

Ditch the chips aisle in the supermarket. Ultra-processed foods are bad for your health and waistline. They often include artificial additives and are rich in sugar, salt, and starch. Eating a diet high in processed foods makes you more prone to obesity, diabetes, and heart disease. Ultra-processed foods are also designed to be addictive, making them hard to put down once you dig in.

Make Meal Prep Pain-Free

Hunching over while peeling that pound of carrots isn't helping your posture or back. Get a kitchen stool or chair to help during longer periods of kitchen prep. Prolonged standing, repetitive motions, and awkward positions while cooking can exacerbate existing back pain and cause new issues. Plan ahead and lay out the ingredients and tools you need to make a meal ahead of time. Take breaks while cooking. Try not to stand still for more than twenty minutes. Maintain good posture, and keep your elbows at a 90-degree angle.

7

Remember Your Meds

Did you take that pill or not? It can be hard to remember in the blur of the morning rush or evening wind-down. If you frequently skip days taking medications or supplements, set an alarm on your phone or leave a sticky note in a prominent place in your home. Make sure you store your medications and supplements in a visible place, and if you have many to take, use a pill box. Many medications need to be taken at the same time. Leave your pill box or bottle near a spot you frequent in the morning or evening—next to your toothbrush or coffee maker. Once you've taken your pills, turn the bottle upside down so you know they've been taken.

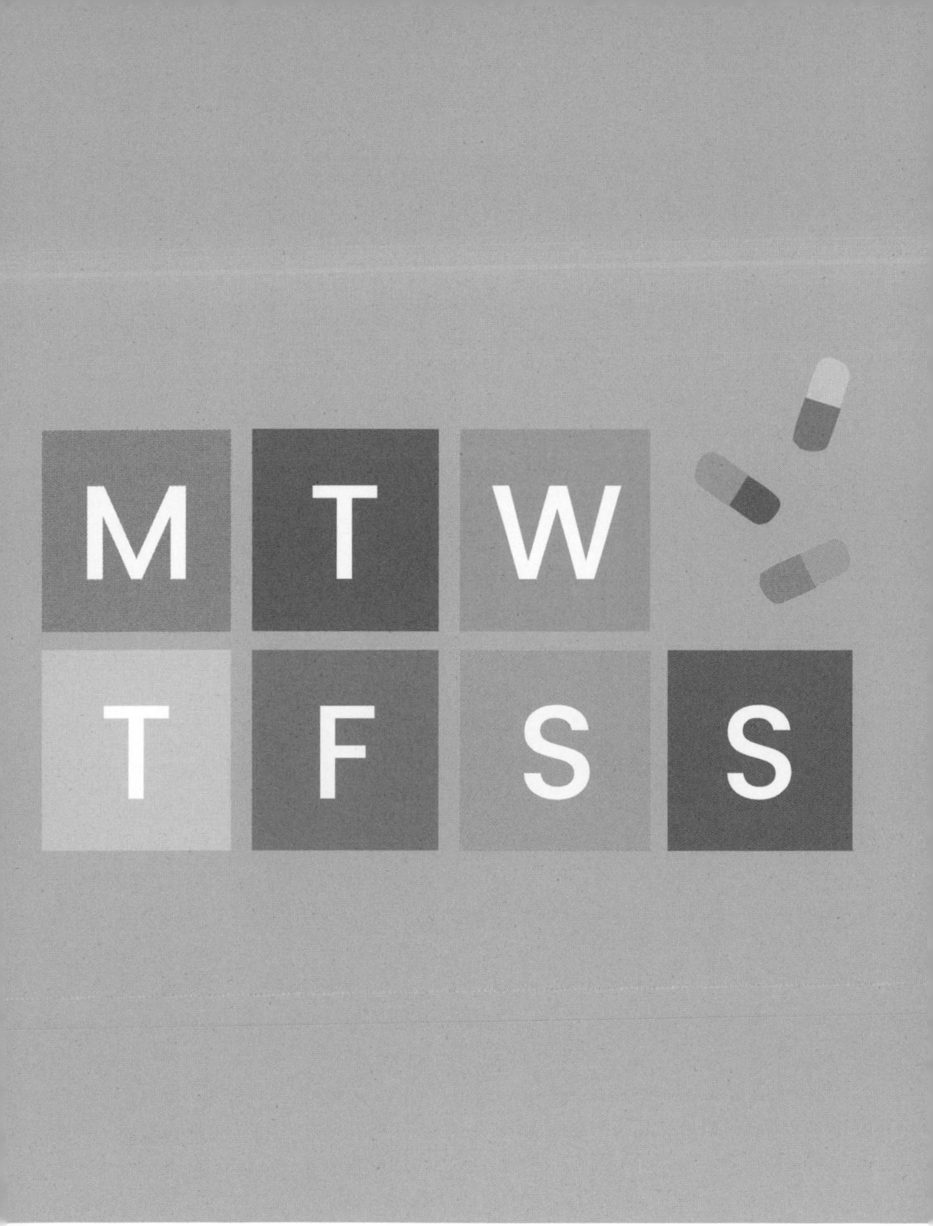
M T W
T F S S

8

Get Your Plank On

Even if you don't have time to exercise, do plank exercises every day. Planks are great for building up core and back muscles, which improves posture and helps prevent injuries from other exercises. If you need to, start with your knees on the floor. Once you progress to doing it with knees up, focus on doing multiple sets up to thirty seconds. You can extend up to a minute but don't exceed two minutes. Once you can comfortably do a plank for a minute, incorporate other variations—such as leg lifts—while in a plank.

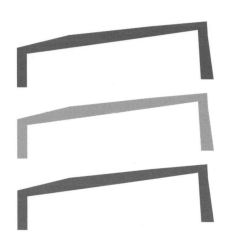

9

Brush Your Tongue

Your dentist has probably told you many times: brush your teeth twice a day and floss once a day. (Who *really* flosses daily?) But brushing your tongue can also improve dental hygiene if you suffer from bad breath. Bacteria accumulates on your tongue and can contribute to bad breath. Brush your tongue when you brush your teeth, or you can also get a tongue scraper.

Wear Earplugs

Scored tickets to Taylor Swift's concert? Consider wearing ear protection at the concert. Noise that exceeds 70 decibels over a sustained time period can damage your hearing. Noise above 120 decibels causes immediate harm. Wear ear protection when you are doing activities that could damage hearing, which includes using a lawnmower or leaf blower, or yes, attending a loud concert or sporting event.

11

Swish and Spit

If you're looking for a fix for long-lasting bad breath, look for a therapeutic rather than cosmetic mouthwash. Therapeutic mouthwashes—which can be bought over the counter or by prescription—attack the bacteria that cause bad breath but may also reduce tooth plaque, inflammation of the gums, and tooth decay.

12

Veg Up

Find creative ways to sneak in those veggies. Bake carrots or zucchini into your favorite muffins or breads. Swap out mashed potatoes for mashed cauliflower. Substitute half of the ground meat in your burgers with some hearty mushrooms. Shredded vegetables can be added to anything without much notice, even pancakes. Aim to get five portions of vegetables and fruit a day.

Shop Online for Groceries

We all know the siren call of the candy bars and other junk food clustered around the front of the grocery store. Avoid the temptation of impulse purchases by shopping for groceries online. Plot your meals for the week, and schedule a weekly delivery for the weekend. Overweight people trying to lose weight who did their grocery shopping online purchased fewer high-fat foods and less food overall, according to one study.

Moisturize

Find the right moisturizer for your skin type, whether it's dry, oily, or combination. One way to do this is to press blotting sheets, which absorb oil, to a clean face. A simpler way is to observe your face thirty minutes after washing it. If it's tight and flaky, you have dry skin. If it's shiny, you likely have oily skin. And if it's shiny just on your forehead or nose area, you may have combination skin. Try to apply moisturizer once or twice a day, ideally after a shower or bath when your skin is moist to lock in the water. Look for a hypoallergenic, fragrance-free moisturizer to avoid unnecessary chemicals.

Try a NEAT and Tidy Workout

Vacuuming, mopping, and carrying loads of laundry up and down the stairs may seem like a nuisance. But what if it also counts as your workout? Cleaning chores can burn a significant amount of calories, referred to as NEAT, or non-exercise activity thermogenesis, which is the calories we burn with day-to-day activities. Take on chores you might outsource, like mowing the lawn or gardening. You can make cleaning more of a workout by incorporating simple movements. Do push-ups in between folding clothes. Incorporate squats while you scrub the bathrooms. Try some lunges as you vacuum or mop. Now you've done resistance training and cardio and have a clean house to boot.

Eat Your Vitamins

Vitamin C and collagen supplements may be all the rage, but you likely don't need them. Our bodies absorb nutrients better from whole foods. It's healthier to get your vitamin C from an orange than a supplement. Same goes for other nutrients. Get your calcium from dairy, and iron from leafy greens, meat, or legumes. You'll save some money too.

Breakfast for Dinner

It's been a long day, and the last thing you want to do is come up with something to cook for dinner. Enter breakfast for dinner. Whip up an omelette and be sure to add a bunch of veggies. Add some whole wheat toast, and you have yourself a healthy dinner in a pinch. Oatmeal topped with fruit also works well. Just save the pancakes for dessert.

Skip the Elevator

Don't have time for a workout today? That's OK—just take the stairs whenever you can. You may not think climbing up or down a few flights of stairs is a lot, but it adds up. Going up or even down stairs burns calories, improves your heart health over time, and may even reduce the risk of stroke. Taking the stairs also improves leg power and helps maintain healthy bones and muscles.

19

Shovel Carefully

Use caution when shoveling snow, especially if you have heart and back problems. Shoveling snow increases your heart rate and blood pressure, placing a big burden on the heart. The cold air can also impact your heart by causing the arteries to constrict. Even if you don't have cardiovascular issues, try to reduce your shoveling effort to about 80 percent and take frequent breaks. Avoid eating a heavy meal thirty to sixty minutes before shoveling as that can place an extra load on the heart. Also, put a scarf over your mouth to prevent breathing in too much cold air. To avoid back problems, bend your knees while shoveling and aim to push the snow rather than lift it.

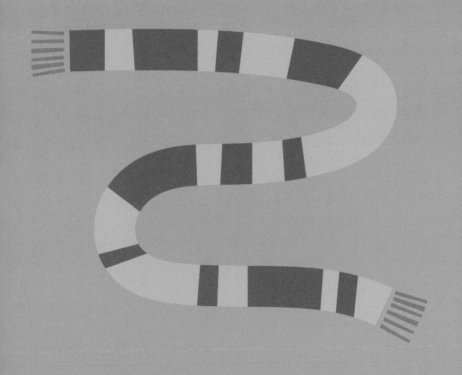

Berry Good

Add a half cup of strawberries or blueberries to your morning smoothie two to three times a week. It's good for your physical health and helps preserve your cognitive health. Berries are high in antioxidants and are linked to reducing the risk of developing Alzheimer's disease.

Peep at Your Pee

Take a peek after you finish in the bathroom. If your pee is dark, you may not be drinking enough water. It's important to stay well hydrated, and while all liquids help do that, H_2O is the best. Start your day with a tall, refreshing glass of water. It's free, zero calories, and good for maintaining proper hydration, aiding digestion, and replacing fluids lost through sweating and activity. If you're not a big fan of the taste of water, enhance your beverage with fruit infusions or herbs, or try a sparkling version. There's no hard and fast rule about how much water to drink a day. It depends on your size, your activity level, and the climate you live in. But try to make the majority of your fluid intake water.

Pump Down the Volume

Use an app to monitor the sound intensity of the music you listen to. Exposure to loud noises can be damaging to your hearing but also to your overall health. Studies find high noise levels can contribute to heart disease, among other health conditions. If you listen to music at an average level of 90 decibels, limit listening to four hours a week. At 80 decibels you can safely listen to music for up to forty hours a week.

VOLUME

Walk the Walk

Schedule walking segments into your day. Park your car in the farthest spot of your office's parking lot or change the venue for a business meeting. Go for a stroll with your colleagues, and get down to business in a park rather than a fluorescent-lit conference room.

Walking is an easy way to meet the 150 minutes of physical activity a week recommended for health. You don't need to tackle all two and a half hours at once. Instead try walking in small increments. This may mean leaving for work ten minutes earlier or walking to get your lunch. Bonus if you take that walk with a friend to get the added benefits of socialization. Even if you don't reach the 150-minute threshold of walking, there are still benefits to less walking. Walking just eleven minutes a day (along with any other type of moderate physical activity) increases longevity.

Get the Most from Your Joe

There's nothing quite like that first cup of coffee in the morning. It wakes us up, comforts us, and gets us ready for the day. Coffee includes some good things, too, like antioxidants that can reduce inflammation. Caffeine is OK in moderation, but it can also be addictive and lead to mental disorders including caffeine intoxication and withdrawal. However, three to five cups of coffee per day is acceptable and even associated with a lower risk of heart disease and cancer. But some people are more sensitive to caffeine and metabolize it much slower. If this is you, then try to avoid drinking coffee in the afternoon and evening.

Avoid coffee and other caffeinated products if you have conditions such as high blood pressure, insomnia, and anxiety. If you feel jittery or restless after drinking coffee, that is a red flag. Mix caffeinated and decaffeinated drinks and gradually cut back on the amount of caffeine you consume in a week by about 25 percent to avoid withdrawal symptoms, such as bad headaches. If you don't want to eliminate it completely, try to drink it in small doses at irregular intervals.

Blue Light Begone

Those cute animal videos on TikTok can wait until tomorrow. Stop doomscrolling through videos and social media feeds before bedtime, and avoid the computer and television too. Your backlit smartphone emits blue light, which interferes with your sleep. Blue light suppresses the release of the hormone melatonin, which makes you sleepy at night. Avoid screens an hour or two before bedtime. If that's not realistic you can try using a blue-light screen filter on your phone or computer or blue-light blocking glasses. Most electronic devices have nighttime modes, and you can also manually reduce the brightness.

Bottoms Down

Get over your New Year's hangover by trying Dry January. We all know drinking alcohol raises our risk for numerous types of cancer as well as a host of other health issues. Dry January, a popular movement that started in the United Kingdom and has spread to the United States, entails abstaining from alcohol for a month. Opt for sparking water, no-alcohol beers, or mocktails when you're at happy hour. A one-month break from alcohol leaves people with better sleep, three to four pounds lighter, and with improved health markers, such as lower blood pressure, lower insulin resistance, and improved liver function. There are benefits even if you don't succeed in going dry for the whole month. People report cutting back on how much they drink alcohol up to six months later whether they made it through the whole month or not.

Sleep on a Schedule

Getting seven to nine hours of shut-eye is important, but it's just as important to be on a regular sleep schedule. Try to maintain a regular sleep schedule by going to bed and waking up at roughly the same time every day, including weekends. This means not feeling bad if you need to skip a late-night Saturday party. And don't try to make up for weekday sleep deficits on the weekends by dozing until noon. Aim for not varying these times by more than an hour if you can.

Be a Home Cook

Take an hour on Sundays to cut up vegetables to roast and have on hand for dinner during the week. Get some proteins ready, too, by hard-boiling eggs and cooking beans or chicken that you can use for multiple meals. Prepare a batch of overnight oats. Just an hour of your weekend will make it less likely that you'll resort to takeout or eating out. Eating at home is both easier on the wallet and the stomach. People who cook at home have healthier diets and spend less on food. They eat more fruits and vegetables and adhere more to a Mediterranean diet. Once you're cooking more at home, freeze leftovers—like soups and sauces—to make your future days of prep even easier.

Go See the Doc

Going to the doctor is no one's idea of fun. But staying up to date on your doctor's appointments is an important part of catching health issues early and preventing new ones from developing. The screenings and vaccinations you need depend on your age, gender, and family and personal history. Wellness appointments are a good time to check in with a doctor on any health concerns, get a blood pressure screening, and make sure you're up to date on vaccinations.

In your twenties: Get the HPV vaccine to protect against human papillomaviruses, which cause many cervical and other cancers, if you didn't get it as an adolescent. The U.S. Centers for Disease Control and Prevention recommends getting the vaccine through the age of twenty-six. Get tested for sexually transmitted diseases like gonorrhea, chlamydia, and HIV. You should also get tested for hepatitis C once in your lifetime. Screenings for cervical cancer—typically a pap smear—in women of average risk are

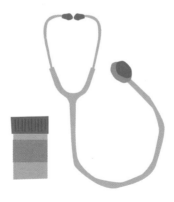

recommended starting at age twenty-one through age sixty-five every three years. This is also a good time to get the hepatitis B vaccine, which protects against liver cancer and other liver damage, if you haven't already.

In your thirties: Start thinking about getting screened for diabetes. Some groups recommend screening for prediabetes and type 2 diabetes starting at age thirty-five in people who are overweight or have obesity. But others recommend that all adults older than thirty-five get screened for type 2 diabetes (they recommend that those with risk factors get tested earlier).

In your forties: Get your cholesterol levels checked to see if you need to take a statin, a cholesterol-lowering medication. Women at average risk for breast cancer should start getting mammograms for breast cancer at least every two years. And men and women should get a colorectal cancer screening at age forty-five. If you don't have glasses or contacts or don't regularly see an eye doctor, this is a good time to see one to get a baseline screening for eye diseases such as glaucoma and cataracts.

In your fifties: Get the shingles vaccine. Women who have reached menopause should get screened for osteoporosis if they are at high risk for fractures. Lung cancer screenings are recommended for adults fifty to eighty years old who have a twenty pack-year smoking history and currently smoke or quit within the past fifteen years. (Lifetime exposure to smoking is often quantified in pack-years. A twenty pack-year history is equivalent to smoking a pack a day for twenty years or the equivalent, such as two packs a day for ten years). Starting at age fifty, men of average risk should talk to a health care provider about the pros and cons of screening for prostate cancer.

In your sixties: If you're over sixty-five, the CDC recommends getting the pneumonia vaccine. Women sixty-five and older should get screened for osteoporosis.

30

Digital Strain

The average adult spends roughly seven hours per day in front of a screen. The constant glare of screens gets to our eyes. Thankfully, there are ways to reduce digital eye strain, sometimes referred to as computer vision syndrome, which results from looking at screens for long periods of time without taking a break. This can result in blurry vision, dry eyes, and headaches.

- Follow the twenty-twenty-twenty rule. For every twenty minutes you are looking at a computer or cell phone screen, look at something twenty feet away for at least twenty seconds.

- Blink twelve to fifteen times a minute. When we stare at a computer screen we blink as little as five to seven times a minute.

- Reduce the glare on your screen and adjust the brightness. You can try a screen glare filter or position your screen away from windows and bright lights.

- Place your computer screen at a slightly lower level and roughly twenty to twenty-eight inches from your eyes.

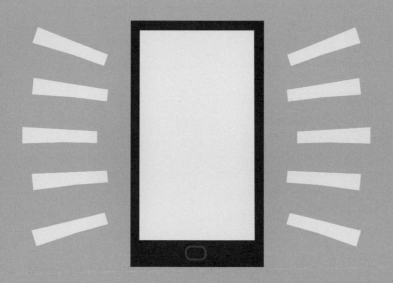

Sleep Cool

Turn the thermostat down. To fall asleep, your core body temperature needs to drop by about 2 to 3 degrees Fahrenheit.

- A good temperature for sleep is 65 degrees Fahrenheit. If you're piling on the blankets you can drop it lower.

- Taking a hot bath or shower before going to bed helps drop your core body temperature by bringing circulating blood to the surface of the body.

- Wear light cotton clothing to bed and use layers of bedding so you can take them off as needed.

- We lose heat from our hands and feet so put on socks in bed if you're feeling cold. If you're hot, stick your hands and/or feet out of the covers.

Pump Up the Iron

Runners: make time for resistance training. Many of us focus on cardiovascular exercise, which is important, but some form of weight lifting or weight-bearing exercise is increasingly important as we age. We lose 10 percent of our muscle mass every decade. Strength training can help counteract that by preserving and improving muscle mass. Having more lean muscle mass can also increase your metabolism and help burn calories. And you don't need to hit the gym to get some sessions in. Strength training can be done at home with the help of free weights or resistance bands. If you don't have equipment you can even use something as simple as canned food, or stick to exercises that use your body weight, such as push-ups, squats, and planks. Aim for twelve to fifteen repetitions per set. Do strength training for twenty to thirty minutes, at least two times a week. And be sure to have a rest day before you work the same muscles again.

Power Naps

Get on board with the European tradition of a daytime siesta. Getting some sleep during the day can be beneficial to your health. Naps can reduce daytime sleepiness, improve your work performance, and enhance athletic abilities. Reap the most benefit from daytime naps:

- Don't nap so late that it interferes with becoming tired at night. Think post-lunch, some time between 1:00 and 4:00 p.m.

- Nap for no longer than ten to twenty minutes.

- Set an alarm or sleep upright if you want to ensure you don't snooze for too long.

- Drink a caffeinated beverage before napping to help with the grogginess that sometimes lingers post-nap.

Stand, Don't Sit

Consider a standing desk when you work. Sitting is bad for your health and posture. Sitting for extended periods of time—which we are all guilty of—increases the risk of just about every chronic condition, including cancer, heart disease, and diabetes, not to mention potential muscle aches. Sitting for extended periods of time also causes calories to be stored as fat rather than muscle, while standing burns roughly 10 percent more calories than sitting. Break up sedentary behavior by standing for at least a couple of minutes for roughly every twenty minutes or so you sit. Move at least two of the eight hours you're at work.

Save Your Skin

The sun is not our skin's friend as it contributes to the risk of developing skin cancer. Be sure to apply sunscreen at least thirty minutes before you head outside even if it's a cloudy or gray day. Reapply it every one to two hours or after swimming or sweating to protect your skin from damaging sun rays that contribute to the risk of developing skin cancer. Look for a broad-spectrum sunscreen that will protect your skin from ultraviolet rays, both UVA and UVB, with a sun protection factor (SPF) of thirty or higher. Try to avoid going outside in the sun when the rays are especially intense. At the beach cover yourself with long-sleeve swim shirts, pants, sunglasses, and broad-brimmed hats.

Vary Your Exercise Routine

No matter what your exercise routine is, it's a good idea to change things up when you can. Our bodies get used to doing the same exercises and using the same muscles in the same way to the point where you start burning fewer calories. If you try a different type of exercise your body will have to work harder and burn more calories. Swapping running for, say, swimming also helps prevent overuse injuries and could work new muscles. Shaking things up can also help boredom with your exercise routine. Try a dance class instead of yoga, or go on a hike rather than running on the treadmill.

Find the Light

Rise and shine and get some morning sunshine if you can. It's important to expose yourself to bright light in the morning because it signals to the body that it's time to wake up and it helps you feel alert. It also suppresses the hormone melatonin, which makes you sleepy. That early morning sunshine will also help you become sleepy in the evening when it's time to go to sleep. Ideally you should go outside to get natural sunlight (good for vitamin D too!), but if it's dark or there's no natural light you can try using a 10,000-lux light box, which mimics outdoor light, within an hour of waking up for at least twenty to thirty minutes.

38

Wear Shades

No, you don't need to wear your sunglasses at night, but don't forget them during the day. The sun's rays aren't just harmful to our skin; they can damage our eyes too. Sunglasses can protect your eyes. Make sure your sunglasses have a UV400 rating or say "100% UV protection." If you have tinted glasses, make sure they have UV protection. Wraparound frames that cover your entire eye are good. Even if you have UV-blocking contact lenses, wear sunglasses. Wearing a wide-brimmed hat also helps.

Stretch

Stretching after a workout is a great way to prevent injuries and increase flexibility. But stretching every day is good for your body even if you don't exercise. It can be especially helpful in the morning to wake up your body and get the blood flowing, but it can also help relax your muscles before bedtime. Stretching helps maintain your range of motion and keeps muscles flexible and strong. This helps prevent muscle injuries from sudden movements and loosens tight muscles. Stretching can also help improve joint or muscle pain and helps with balance. Hold each stretch for thirty to sixty seconds. Always stretch both sides of your body and each major muscle group. Don't bounce when you stretch, and stop stretching if you feel pain.

Eat Like the Italians and Greeks

Mangia! The Mediterranean diet has been associated with reducing mortality, lowering the risk of heart disease, and benefiting brain health. Here are some guidelines:

- Focus on healthy fats such as olive oil.

- Eat lots of plant-based foods, such as beans, lentils, nuts, vegetables, and fruits.

- Eat whole-wheat bread and brown rice.

- Eat fish at least two times a week.

- Limit meat intake, particularly red meat, and opt for poultry.

- Limit sweets and butter.

- A glass of red wine with dinner is perfectly fine.

PART TWO

Body
Mind
Spirit

Slow Breaths

Many of us breathe wrong. To start, you should inhale through your nose (not your mouth!) and exhale for longer. You should also breathe slowly, which stimulates the vagus nerve that runs from your brain stem to the abdomen. This can lower the heart rate, aid digestion, and trigger the release of chemicals that have anti-inflammatory effects on the body.

Create and Repeat

Trying to make that thirty-minute exercise routine a habit? Be patient. It takes on average sixty-six days to form a habit. The most difficult part about creating a new routine—whether it's jogging three times a week or getting to sleep earlier—is sticking to it. Simplify the habit you're trying to create and repeat. Try to remove potential obstacles to make it easier and make it fun (think exercising with a friend). It may be challenging initially, but eventually it should become routine.

Create the Perfect Exercise Playlist

Can't figure out what music will motivate you to keep moving? To start, research has found the ideal tempo ranges from 125 to 140 beats per minute. (Think: "Where Did You Go?" by Jax Jones and MNEK). This tempo reduces your perception of exertion. Also, choose songs with encouraging lyrics that reflect your activity (♫♪ Baby, we were born to run ♫♪), which can help you focus and stay positive while you sweat.

Say Cheese!

Smile more, and try to make it a Duchenne smile, which is a genuine smile that creates crow's feet around your eyes. Just the act of smiling may be good for your health, reducing your stress and heart rate. In some studies, people who force a smile using chopsticks have a greater reduction in heart rate after a stressful task than people who have a neutral facial expression. Smiling while getting a shot may also reduce the pain felt from the injection.

Pen to Paper

If you lost a loved one recently or are going through another challenging experience, give journaling a try. Expressive writing—about a traumatic event or one you haven't talked about with others—is especially helpful. Journaling has been shown to strengthen the immune system, reduce pain and inflammation, and improve mood, sleep, and stress levels. Write for fifteen minutes for three or four consecutive days. If you feel better after that, you successfully worked through the challenge.

Digital Decluttering

End your month by cleaning up your inbox, desktop, and photos so you're not drowning in emails and documents. Digital clutter is a source of stress for many people. Clean your inbox in stages. Save important emails and pictures on the same system. Make folders to sort emails by category. Unsubscribe from newsletters or other emails you don't want. Make sure your photos are saved to iCloud or somewhere other than the device they're stored on. Do the same for important documents. Organize documents with folders and subfolders. Like physical decluttering, start slow and in increments and try to maintain your digital space by regularly "cleaning up."

Devise a Budget

Being in debt or not having enough money to pay your bills impairs your physical and mental health. Draw up a realistic budget that includes saving money. Set up your direct deposit so a percentage of your paycheck goes directly into a savings account. Avoid buying things you can't afford so you don't have credit card debt. Pinpoint where you're spending too much money, like eating out, and focus on keeping that money within a specified limit. Try using a budgeting app. Be sure to build in money for an occasional splurge when you can.

Set Boundaries

Do you have a colleague who won't stop pinging you about work after hours? Is your boss asking you about a work event when you're on vacation or at your kid's soccer game? It's time to set some boundaries. First figure out your priorities and identify your limits. Then clearly communicate them to your colleagues, friends, and family. Don't feel guilty, and try to be consistent. It's OK to set boundaries at work.

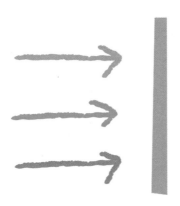

Use Your Commute

Stop doomscrolling or doing work on your commute. Sneak something into your commute that you typically don't have time for. Walk or bike to work to get your exercise in. Listen to a podcast or audiobook if you're driving in the car. Read a book or learn a language from an app if you're on public transportation. Or take a nap if you need to (just not if you're driving!).

50

Curb Your Procrastinating

Instead of perusing your social media accounts while you're trying to write that important memo, set aside time in your day dedicated to looking at social media. Procrastination is the bane of our existence, but time chunking, or reserving blocks of time to complete specific tasks, can help you focus. If it's a large goal, divide it into smaller ones over the course of a week or month. Reward yourself when you meet these goals or subgoals with something as simple as chocolate or a walk.

Be Bored

Being bored doesn't make you uninteresting. Your brain needs rest: boredom gives it that. It also gives you time to allow your mind to wander, which can lead to creativity. Boredom can lead to people solving problems or coming up with new ideas. One study found that people did better trying to come up with excuses for being late after a boring task than after crafting. Boredom can also motivate the pursuit of new goals by motivating a desire for change.

Try Bibliotherapy

Switch out your iPhone for a book before you go to sleep. Reading can help prevent cognitive decline. It can reduce stress, feelings of loneliness, and other depressive symptoms and can serve as a means of escape if you're going through a difficult time. Reading relaxes the body and can help you fall asleep. Opt for physical books before bedtime as backlight devices can interfere with your sleep. Stay away from reading material that might provoke excitement or anxiety, like nonfiction war books or something that is very difficult to follow. Short stories, novels, or anything that you find relaxing and enjoyable will do.

Banish the Phone

Buy an old-fashioned alarm clock so you don't need to keep your smartphone by your bedside. Charge your phone in a different room or, even better, on a different floor if you live in a multistory house. The temptation to check for texts or notifications or even the time can disrupt your sleep. Looking at content that might be negative or stressful increases levels of the stress hormone cortisol, and even positive news can increase levels of dopamine, a neurotransmitter that can excite parts of the brain. Setting limits on your phone or apps can help prevent you from using them.

Sleep on It

Cramming for a test? Longer naps can have a beneficial role if you have the time to "wake up" from them, as they can leave you groggy for up to thirty minutes. An hour nap leaves enough time for slow-wave sleep—the deepest stage of sleep—so it may help with memory consolidation. One study found that taking a one-hour nap between studying enhanced memory a week later while cramming or taking a break did not.

Clean as You Go

Does a messy space put you in a bad mood? Spend less time cleaning your home by being clean on a day-to-day basis. Regularly sweep the floors and wipe down bathroom surfaces, kitchen counters, and tables. Have a handy, portable vacuum cleaner to quickly clean up spills and messes. Save the deep cleaning for those rainy weekends when you have nothing else to do.

Seek Out Adventure

Go rock climbing, try surfing, or take an improv class! Doing something new and adventurous activates the brain's dopamine system, improving mood and lowering stress levels. You don't have to go skydiving. Anything works if it feels challenging or scary, novel, and out of your comfort zone. If you wimp out when you arrive at that upside-down roller coaster ride, don't get discouraged. It may not be for you, so try something that will be mentally or spiritually adventurous like a silent meditation retreat or a night of karaoke.

Make Your Bed

Buy some comfy linens and maybe that bed sham you've been eyeing. Making your bed will help you get a good night's sleep and make you more motivated to start your day. People who regularly make their bed are more likely to say they got a good night's sleep. Making your bed helps start your day on the right foot with a small accomplishment that may lead to others.

58

Take Small Steps to Meditate

Your first time trying meditation may be a bust. Second time too. Stick with
it and take it slow. Start off with just five minutes. You don't have to sit cross-
legged if it's not comfortable. Find a still, comfortable position for yourself.
Close your eyes, and try to find stillness in your mind. While ideally this will
be in your home at a quiet time, you can meditate anywhere you won't be
disturbed. Using an app or music can help if you're somewhere with outside
sounds. Once you've mastered a five-minute meditation practice, gradually
increase the time as you can. Studies show meditation and mindfulness
practices can lower stress levels and blood pressure and can help people
with chronic conditions handle pain and depression. Research suggests that
meditation may even alter the structure of the brain.

Commit to a Lunch Break

Avoid eating lunch at your desk whether you're working in the office or at home. Having a short break from work leads to greater productivity and job satisfaction. It can promote team building with the people you work with and prevent burnout. A short walk to your food destination or eating outdoors will enhance the break. Bringing lunch from home can make it a healthier meal and is cost efficient. But don't eat your home-cooked meal at your desk. Rather, enjoy it outside with a colleague. You may not have time to do this every day, but aim for a real lunch break at least twice a week.

Stop Multitasking

Don't edit that memo when you're on a conference call about a different topic. You may think you're getting more done by juggling dual tasks. But you're not. Multitasking does not make us more efficient. It can make us less productive and more prone to mistakes, leading to unnecessary stress. Our brains are designed to do one task at a time. The right and left side of the brain's prefrontal cortex work together when you're doing a task that demands attention. If you're distracted by another task, however, the two sides have to work separately, which increases the chance of mistakes and can make you less productive. It's best to limit distractions while you're completing a task and focus solely on what you're doing.

Tame Your To-Do List

Scheduling that doctor's appointment, giving away those bags of old clothes, and cleaning out the pantry are hanging over your head. Add them to your to-do list. Having a to-do list can help remove some of the emotional and mental burden that we all get from unfinished tasks. Physically adding something to your to-do list makes you more aware of what you need and want to get done and may make you more likely to get it done. And there is great satisfaction in checking something off your to-do list. Make sure your list includes practical things you can get done. If a goal is too big or lofty—such as write a book!—break it down into smaller parts. List items by priority and importance with the ASAPs at the top. Keep your list in a visible place, like on the fridge, include a reminder that pops up on your phone, or tack the list to your desk.

Find a Work Spouse

Find a work wife, husband, or significant other. It will make you happier and more committed to your work. And it doesn't matter if you're married or in a committed relationship. Having a work spouse or partner is a strictly platonic relationship defined by a close bond in which two people support, trust, and confide in each other. This is especially important in today's high-pressure environment, which can be ultracompetitive and even toxic at times.

Turn Good Behaviors into Great Habits

Try to make habits out of behaviors you seek to do regularly, like exercise or food prep.

- Make them specific goals, for instance by exercising at a specific time of day for a specific amount of time.

- Research shows using cues can help, so schedule things before or after something that's already part of your routine.

- Make it fun by playing your favorite playlist or rewarding yourself with something when you're done.

- Surrounding yourself with others who are of a like mind can help.

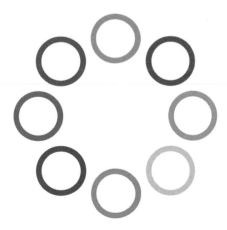

Bonjour, Hola, Ni hao!

Make your high school French teacher proud. Brush up on that second or third language you took in high school or college and haven't spoken since, or try learning an entirely new language. It may be harder to learn a language as you get older but it's great for your brain—parts of your brain even grow! People who speak more than one language have more gray matter in their brains than those who speak one language, which means better memory skills. If you don't have a lot of time then start practicing with an app. You can also take a class or do a one-hour conversational meetup with a fluent speaker. Consider traveling to the country where the language is spoken so you can chat with natives. Also, learn the words for your favorite foods so you can order at restaurants.

Go Old-School with a Board Game

Instead of whiling away your free time with solo games of Candy Crush or video games, dust off your old versions of Scrabble, Monopoly, or Pictionary. Better yet, try some of the more challenging newer games like Settlers of Catan or an old classic, chess. Board games alleviate cognitive impairment and depression. More important, playing board games helps keep us off screens and increases social connections.

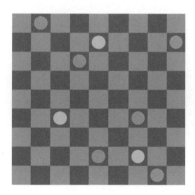

Become a Plant Fanatic

Monsteras, succulents, money trees—take your pick. Houseplants can boost your mood and enhance health. One study found that people who repotted a houseplant reported feeling calmer and had a reduction in blood pressure compared to when doing a computer task. Plants can also improve indoor air quality and may even boost your work performance.

Try, also, getting plants that serve a dual purpose, such as producing a pleasant smell, or herbs or small vegetables that can be used in cooking. Indoor plants that don't require a lot of sunlight or care, or ones that can be replanted, such as spider plants or succulents, may work best. Build time in your day to nurture your budding relationships.

Marie Kondo Your Life

Be ruthless about decluttering your space. Having an organized space reduces stress and makes us feel less anxious. Clutter can also have a negative impact on mental health. Start simple and slow when tackling decluttering. Pick one room or closet. And don't head to a store to buy more items like storage boxes and shelves to help you organize. The goal is to reduce and eliminate things, not acquire more. Save the sentimental stuff—like children's artwork and knickknacks from family vacations—for last. Try donating or giving away your eliminated stuff to a charity or through a Buy Nothing group for an extra boost of happiness. On birthdays and holidays, ask for experiential gifts—tickets to a concert or a meal out at a special restaurant—rather than physical objects.

Vote

It doesn't matter what your political party is, voting is good for your health. People who vote report eating healthier and having less depressive symptoms than those who don't. Voting leaves us with a sense of empowerment and a feeling that we can make a change. It's good for our mental health and makes us feel like we're part of a community.

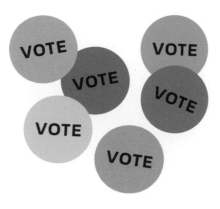

Make Yourself a Mix

Make a playlist of your favorite songs. Play it in the morning while in the shower, at breakfast, or on your commute to work. Music engages the brain and can reduce anxiety, pain, and blood pressure. It also triggers positive memories and improves your mood. Make different mixes from different periods of your life and to evoke a variety of emotions. Try a mix of songs from your childhood or teenage years for when you want to wax nostalgic. Make a sad mix for when you're feeling down and want to wallow a bit and an uplifting mix for when you want to dance around the kitchen. Make a mix that reminds you of your partner and one that harkens to your college days.

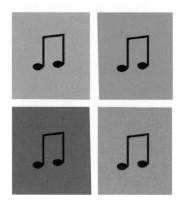

Take a Mental Health Day, but Choose Your Adventure

Feeling anxious and overwhelmed? It's time for a mental health day. Step back and recenter yourself. Don't just lie in bed and doomscroll or binge-watch Netflix. Here are some possibilities:

- **The Chill Mental Health Day:** Take time for yourself by doing something you find relaxing and enjoy—a movie plus a solo lunch at your favorite restaurant with a book, or a yoga class followed by a massage and a nap on your couch.

- **The Social Mental Health Day:** Spend some quality time with a friend or family member.

- **The Productive Mental Health Day:** Get to that doctor's appointment you've been putting off, and run those errands you never seem to have time to get to. Or use the day, uninterrupted, to clean out your closets or the garage.

- **The Personal Challenge Mental Health Day:** Take that ten-mile run you've been training for, or cook the elaborate dinner that will definitely take you all day to prepare.

PART THREE

Body
Mind
Spirit

Take Up a New Hobby

Try a cooking class. Sign up for tennis lessons. Paint. Studies show people with hobbies have better physical and mental health, less stress, and better social connections. Better yet, make it something new you haven't tried before. Learning new skills or activities is good for brain health and preserving your cognitive skills. One study found that when older people were assigned to different activities for three months, they performed better on memory tests up to a year later compared to people who were watching movies or playing games and were not as mentally challenged.

Hug It Out

Give someone a hug with crisscrossed arms for about five to ten seconds. This is the ideal hug, according to research. Hugging is good for ourselves and others. It reduces stress levels and may even reduce your likelihood of getting sick. The longer the hug, the better. Just don't make it so long that it's awkward. And you don't need another person to reap the benefits. Even hugging yourself can reduce stress hormones. And yes, hugging your pets counts too.

Widen Your Social Circle

Don't spend all your time with the same people. People who have social interactions with a more diverse set of relationship types are happier. So instead of having ten conversations a day with your partner and kids, try swapping some of those for a chat with a friend or acquaintance. Taking a class, joining a gym, or volunteering are all ways you can meet different people.

Date Yourself

Make a date. With yourself. Pick your favorite activity, whether it's curling up on the couch with a martini to rewatch your favorite flick or going to an art museum to see your favorite exhibit. Make it special by dressing up if you're going out and indulge in your favorite food or drink. And don't forget to toast yourself—you are worth it.

75

Make a Mindful Dinner

Have the weekday blahs? Why not make mealtime special?

- Light some candles or buy flowers as a centerpiece.

- Play your favorite music.

- Keep your phone out of it. Eat in the kitchen, ideally with the people you live with.

- Spend at least twenty minutes on your meal. Savor and reflect on your food and each bite.

- Eat slowly so you can acknowledge the satiety hormones communicating between your brain and stomach. Chew your food thoroughly and put your utensils down between bites.

Nature Bathing

Immerse yourself in nature. Try twenty minutes of walking in the woods or even a garden. What do you smell? Can you touch the bark of a tree or some moss? Notice the flowers and plants around you and the sounds of the birds and breeze. Meditate, sit, or stroll. The Japanese notion of "forest bathing," which entails spending quiet time in the forest and surrendering to its sounds and smell, is linked to a whole host of health benefits, including reducing depression and anxiety symptoms, lowering stress hormones, and reducing blood pressure level and heart rate. A trip to a forest is even linked to an increase in anticancer proteins and cells.

Shake It Up

Be spontaneous and go to dinner in a neighborhood you've never been to. People whose movements are more unpredictable are happier, according to research. There may even be positive brain changes to being adventurous. Brain scans of a subset of the participants in one study found that those who roamed the most had the best connections between the hippocampus— a region of the brain important for memory, stress regulation, and mood—and regions of the brain important for reward and positive emotion.

Vaca-yay!-tion

Honey, pack your bathing suit and hat, we're heading to Hawaii! Vacations are linked to reducing stress, the risk of heart attacks, and depression, and can lead to improved work performance. Women who take more vacations are less likely to report feeling depressed or tired and are more satisfied with their marriages. And vacations don't have to be long to reap the benefits. The benefits from vacation peak on the eighth day before gradually declining. Just the act of planning a vacation can improve mood. But unfortunately the afterglow from a vacation doesn't last long: most of us are back to baseline within a week. So taking shorter, more frequent vacations is a good goal.

Get a Pet

Waking up at the crack of dawn to walk your dog in a downpour of rain isn't exactly fun. But while dogs and other pets are a big responsibility, they also come with many health benefits. Dog owners who walk their dogs get the health benefits that come with regular exercise and being outdoors. They also often socialize with other dog owners. Dogs and other pets can help people—especially the elderly who may live alone—feel less lonely. Pets also help people of all ages feel less anxiety and depression symptoms. Having a pet is also linked to decreases in blood pressure and cholesterol levels, as well as levels of the stress hormone cortisol, and improved mood. If you don't have a dog or pet, consider volunteer work at a shelter or dog-sitting your friend's dog while they're away.

Ask for Help

Need childcare or meal help or someone to talk to? Acknowledge when you need help or support, and don't be afraid to ask for it. Most people want to help others in need, and it helps them too. It may feel uncomfortable at first, but start with small requests from people you trust and have helped out in the past. Be honest about what you're going through and why you may need the help, and be sure to reciprocate with offers of help when someone else is in need.

Compliment Away

Pay someone a compliment. It can be something as simple and specific as complimenting your cashier's blouse to telling a colleague they did a great job with a presentation or letting a friend know that they're a great listener. Complimenting people lifts their mood—and yours.

Exercise with Friends

Friends that sweat together stay together, so get an exercise buddy or take a group exercise class. Exercising with someone whose company you enjoy makes working out something to look forward to and will make you more accountable and less likely to skip days. It also can make you work harder. And while there are health benefits whether you are exercising alone or with a group, there's some evidence that those who exercise more often with others are in better health.

Practice Positive Self-Talk

We try not to compare our children to others, so stop comparing yourself to your do-it-all neighbor. Talk to yourself the way you want others to talk to you. Strive to feel as kind and loving to yourself as you are with your loved ones. Acknowledging mistakes and being patient with yourself can lower your stress levels. Rather than beating yourself up over something, step back and take a broader, realistic view. Self-compassion can increase motivation and increase happiness. So seek to keep your inner voice kind and compassionate.

Stay Connected

Try to make your connections more than digital. Watching your friends' and family's lives unfold on social media is not the same as maintaining a friendship. Keep in touch with your family and close friends, particularly elderly folks. Loneliness can negatively impact health, raising the risk of many chronic diseases, including diabetes, stroke, and Alzheimer's disease. Studies have found a lack of social connections has a similar impact on mortality as smoking fifteen cigarettes a day. Make an effort to see people in person or have a telephone conversation or Facetime call if they live far away. When that's not possible, a text or email are also ways to remain connected. If someone close to you lives far away, try to see them when you're traveling for work or plot vacations or road trips near where they live, when possible.

Find the Silver Lining

Try to remain hopeful even when things don't go your way. You don't have to be a Pollyanna, but having a sunny, glass-half-full outlook on life helps. Optimistic people tend to be happier and healthier. It's impossible to always be optimistic, and sometimes focusing on negative feelings can help us figure out what is bothering us. But when you can, find the silver lining when things don't go the way you anticipated. Focus on cherishing the small things in life, whether it's your daily cup of tea or when your favorite song comes on the radio.

86

Click, Click, Click!

Snap away on your next vacation, concert, or fancy dinner. The act of taking photos actually enhances your enjoyment of an experience and boosts your engagement. Even taking selfies can improve mood. One study found that regularly taking selfies and sharing them with friends can make you happier.

Pay It Forward

Pay your friend a compliment. Offer your seat to an elderly person. Buy your colleague a cup of coffee. Random acts of kindness are more powerful than you may realize. Research shows that people underestimate their effect, which may hold them back from performing them. Kindness and generosity are also contagious. Choose a day and go on a kindness spree, as research finds multiple gestures in a small window of time provide maximum benefits. One study found people saw a greater boost in happiness if they did five acts of kindness in one day rather than over the course of a week.

88

Be Kind

Acts of kindness don't just benefit others. They benefit you. Psychologists refer to this as prosocial behavior. Such behavior protects against the negative effects of stress. Being kind lowers blood pressure and the stress hormone cortisol and can improve mood. Kindness boosts levels of the neurotransmitters dopamine and serotonin, which are in the reward centers of your brain, and oxytocin, the feel-good hormone that helps connect people.

89

Unplug

Enough with TikTok and YouTube. Put your phone down.

- Go on a hike or bike ride, or go to a museum. Try focusing on people, relationships, and activities that don't involve your phone or screens.

- Ban screens during meals, whether you're eating alone or with your family.

- Try to limit screen use in your bedroom, especially before bed.

- Try to have a screen-free day. If that's not practical, limit your social media use. Limiting your social media use to thirty minutes a day may even reduce loneliness and depression symptoms.

- Avoid looking at your phone too much when you're at a party or hanging out with friends or family.

Cherish Your Friends

Having a large network of friends is good for your physical and mental health and may even trump having a partner or close circle of relatives. According to one study that followed older people over ten years, the people with many friends were less likely to die during that time period than those with few friends. Another study found that middle-aged men were less likely to have a heart disease if they had support from an extended network of friends, whereas having close contacts played less of a role. Here are some ways to maintain friendships:

- Have regularly scheduled times to meet with your friends, whether it's a walking date, a book club meeting, a potluck dinner, or even a day to do grocery shopping and run errands—together.

- If you live far away from a friend, schedule time to talk to them on the phone or Facetime.

- Don't forget important events in your friends' lives. Mark their birthdays, anniversaries, and kids' birthdays in your calendar, then send them a birthday gift or card. Even texts mean a lot to friends.

- If a friend seems distant or absent, ask them how they're feeling. If they're going through a tough time, make sure you check in frequently and see what they need.

Just Say No

No, you don't have to watch your neighbor's dog for the fourth time this year. You can say no! It's hard to decline requests, whether from work or school or a friend. But saying no when you need to is important for self-care, for time management, and to avoid burnout. It's also less risky than you think. People don't perceive our "nos" as badly as we might expect them to.

Regift

Feeling guilty about regifting that unused china platter from your mother-in-law? Don't. Regifting is a great way to get rid of clutter, and research shows the recipients of a regift aren't as offended as you'd expect them to be. Surveys show the practice is more widely accepted than taboo, so feel free to shop in your own closets the next time holiday season rolls around, though try to choose items that are in good condition and unused.

Be Grateful

Thanksgiving isn't the only time to be grateful. Start or end your day with a daily gratitude practice. Thinking about or even jotting down a few things you're grateful for every day can improve your physical and mental health. People asked to write weekly about what they were grateful for were happier and more optimistic after ten weeks than a group who were told to write about hassles and another group who wrote about life events. Expressing your gratitude to others can also improve relationships with family, friends, and even coworkers.

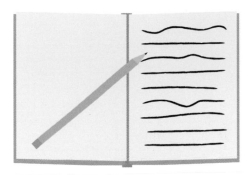

Make Errands Fun

Heading to Costco on a Sunday like half of the neighborhood so you can spend three hours dodging carts and waiting in endless lines? Make errands more enjoyable by listening to that podcast you've been saving or playing an upbeat playlist as you bounce from store to store. Wear a shirt that brings you joy and ask a friend to join you. If you're running errands on a weekend, squeeze a more indulgent chore into the mix, like getting a manicure or facial.

Donate Your Time

It may be tempting to binge-watch a home renovation show in your precious free time. But consider volunteering instead. There are many ways to volunteer, from a one-time shift at a soup kitchen during the holidays to a weekly gig tutoring kids at the local library. Do something you enjoy. If you like parks, participate in a park cleanup. Volunteering even a few hours a month helps both you and your community. It increases positive feelings and reduces stress, and older people who volunteer are in better physical health.

Find Your Inner Picasso

Go ahead, channel that after-work rage by splattering some paint Jackson Pollock–style. Dabbling in art or even looking at it is beneficial in myriad ways. Creating art activates the reward centers of the brain with increased blood flow to those areas. And the benefits from creating art aren't limited to experienced artists. Making art lowers stress and anxiety levels whether you're an experienced artist or an amateur. If you don't want to get your hands dirty, go visit an art museum. People who went to an art museum for just a few hours reported personal, intellectual, social, and physical well-being benefits that lasted days later, or even in some cases months later.

Laugh!

Schitt's Creek or *Seinfeld*? Indulge in whatever tickles your funny bone. A big guffaw activates your parasympathetic nervous system, which causes your body to relax and your blood pressure and heart rate to drop. Laughter also lowers stress hormones and may even increase blood flow. It can also provide pain relief and benefit your immune system. And there's some evidence that those who laugh more have a lower risk of heart disease.

HA HA HA

Free Up Time

Save your laundry for the weekend. Skip your child's third soccer game of the week. Cancel that work dinner. Carve out some free time in the morning and evening to bookend your day. Aim for two hours of free time a day. It doesn't have to be two consecutive hours of free time. People who have less than two hours of free time per day are less happy. But too much free time can backfire. People's happiness starts dropping with more than five hours of free time.

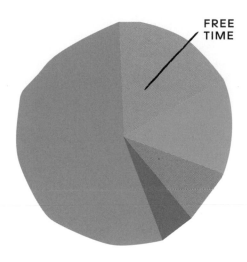

FREE
TIME

Bucket List

Bucket lists are for the living. Write down all your goals, dreams, and desires—and don't censor yourself. Next, separate them into three lists: short-term goals and aspirations that you can complete in the next year or two; medium-term goals that require five to ten years; and long-term dreams that will take you far longer. Mix it up with fun and adventurous activities (think skydiving!), those that require more work and time (reading *War and Peace*, learning to make sushi), and the impressive ones that will require extensive planning and dedication (hiking the Appalachian Trail, living in another country for part of your life). Crossing off items will give you a sense of accomplishment. Feel free to keep adding to your bucket lists, but aim to complete at least one item per year!

Sing!

So what if you can't carry a tune. When "Bohemian Rhapsody" or "Total Eclipse of the Heart" comes on as you're driving on the highway, bring it on. Singing is therapeutic. Singing in a choir is especially beneficial, especially if you're dealing with the recent death of a loved one. It's been shown to help cancer and dementia patients too. Even if you don't have the time or voice to join a choir, just singing your favorite tune in the shower can improve your mood. Or make your own chorus with your family or friends on your next road trip.

ACKNOWLEDGMENTS

Many of the self-care tips in this book came in handy as I was writing this book, my first. I would like to thank my initial editor, Jessica Firger, for coming to me with the idea for this book and encouraging me to take the plunge into book writing. I'd also like to thank my current editor, Caitlin Leffel, who saw the book through to completion. Thanks to the team at Union Square & Co. for publishing the book and my agent, Anna Ghosh of Ghosh Literary, for representing me.

A big thanks to my employer—the *Wall Street Journal*—and all the wonderful editors and reporters I've worked with for more than a decade. I am especially grateful for my current editor, Erin White, and Nikki Waller, the head of our Life & Work group. I am always inspired and in awe of the work of my fellow reporters and columnists at the *Journal* whose great work helped inspire some of these tips. Finally, I want to thank my friends and family for their support and love. This book made me realize all the more how important a supportive community is. So thank you to my friends (a special shout-out to the JHing-bhang!); my parents, Nirmala and Narasimha Reddy; my sister, Sujani Reddy; my husband, Jonathan Rockoff; and my children, Priya and Nikhil, who bring joy and light to my life every day.

BIBLIOGRAPHY

Body

American Optometric Association. "Computer Vision Syndrome." American Optometric Association. 2023. https://www.aoa.org/healthy-eyes/eye-and-vision-conditions /computer-vision-syndrome?sso=y.

Baum, Griffin R., and America's Test Kitchen. *The Healthy Back Kitchen*. Boston: America's Test Kitchen, 2023.

Boyd, Kierstan. "Computers, Digital Devices and Eye Strain." American Academy of Ophthalmology. Updated August 8, 2023. https://www.aao.org/eye-health/tips -prevention/computer-usage.

Buckley, John P., Alan Hedge, Thomas Yates, Robert J. Copeland, Michael Loosemore, Mark Hamer, Gavin Bradley, and David W. Dunstan. "The Sedentary Office: An Expert Statement on the Growing Case for Change towards Better Health and Productivity." *British Journal of Sports Medicine* 49, no. 21 (2015): 1357–62. https://doi.org/10.1136 /bjsports-2015-094618.

Centers for Disease Control and Prevention. "Adult Immunization Schedule by Age." Updated November 16, 2023. https://www.cdc.gov/vaccines/schedules/hcp/imz/adult.html.

Centers for Disease Control and Prevention. "How Much Physical Activity Do Adults Need?" Updated June 2, 2022. https://www.cdc.gov/physicalactivity/basics/adults/index.htm.

Centers for Disease Control and Prevention. "What Noises Cause Hearing Loss?" Updated November 8, 2022. https://www.cdc.gov/nceh/hearing_loss/what_noises_cause_hearing _loss.html.

Chang, Yu-Hung, I-Chien Wu, and Chao A. Hsiung. "Reading Activity Prevents Long-Term Decline in Cognitive Function in Older People: Evidence from a 14-Year Longitudinal Study." *International Psychogeriatrics* 33, no. 1 (2021): 63–74. https://doi.org/10.1017 /s1041610220000812.

de Visser, Richard O., Emily Robinson, and Rod Bond. "Voluntary Temporary Abstinence from Alcohol During 'Dry January' and Subsequent Alcohol Use." *Health Psychology*, 35, no. 3 (2016): 281–289. https://doi.org/10.1037/hea0000297.

Ebben, Matthew R., Peter Yan, and Ana C. Krieger. "The Effects of White Noise on Sleep and Duration in Individuals Living in a High Noise Environment in New York City." *Sleep Medicine* 83 (July 2021): 256–259. https://doi.org/10.1016/j.sleep.2021.03.031.

Garcia, Leandro, Matthew Pearce, Ali Abbas, Alexander Mok, Tessa Strain, Sara Ali, Alessio Crippa, Paddy C. Dempsey, Rajna Golubic, Paul Kelly, et al. "Non-Occupational Physical Activity and Risk of Cardiovascular Disease, Cancer and Mortality Outcomes: A Dose–Response Meta-Analysis of Large Prospective Studies." *British Journal of Sports Medicine* 57, no. 15 (2023). https://doi.org/10.1136/bjsports-2022-105669.

Gorin, Amy A., Hollie A. Raynor, Heather M. Niemeier, and Rena R. Wing. "Home Grocery Delivery Improves the Household Food Environments of Behavioral Weight Loss Participants: Results of an 8-Week Pilot Study." *International Journal of Behavioral Nutrition and Physical Activity* 4 (2007): 58. https://doi.org/10.1186/1479-5868-4-58.

Haghayegh, Shahab, Sepideh Khoshnevis, Michael H. Smolensky, Kenneth R. Diller, and Richard J. Castriotta. "Before-Bedtime Passive Body Heating by Warm Shower or Bath to Improve Sleep: A Systematic Review and Meta-Analysis." *Sleep Medicine Reviews* 46 (August 2019): 124–35. https://doi.org/10.1016/j.smrv.2019.04.008.

Harvard T.H. Chan School of Public Health. "Coffee." The Nutrition Source. Updated July 2020. https://www.hsph.harvard.edu/nutritionsource/food-features/coffee/.

Mehta, Gautam, Stewart Macdonald, Alexandra Cronberg, Matteo Rosselli, Tanya Khera-Butler, Colin Sumpter, Safa Al-Khatib, Anjly Jain, James Maurice, Christos Charalambous, et al. "Short-Term Abstinence from Alcohol and Changes in Cardiovascular Risk Factors, Liver Function Tests and Cancer-Related Growth Factors: A Prospective Observational Study." *BMJ Open* 8, no. 5 (2018). https://doi.org/10.1136/bmjopen-2017-020673.

Moody, Rebecca. "Screen Time Statistics: Average Screen Time in US vs. the Rest of the World." *Comparitech*. March 21, 2022. https://www.comparitech.com/tv-streaming/screen-time-statistics/.

Murphy, Stephen, Tim Hill, Pierre McDonagh, and Amanda Flaherty. "Mundane Emotions: Losing Yourself in Boredom, Time and Technology." *Marketing Theory* 23, no. 2 (November 2022): 275–293. https://doi.org/10.1177/14705931221138617.

The Skin Cancer Foundation. "Sun Protection." Updated June 2021. https://www.skincancer.org/skin-cancer-prevention/sun-protection/.

U.S. Food and Drug Administration. "Tips to Stay Safe in the Sun: From Sunscreen to Sunglasses." Updated August 15, 2022. https://www.fda.gov/consumers/consumer -updates/tips-stay-safe-sun-sunscreen-sunglasses.

Windred, Daniel P., Angus C. Burns, Jacqueline M. Lane, Richa Saxena, Martin K. Rutter, Sean W. Cain, and Andrew J. K. Phillips. "Sleep Regularity Is a Stronger Predictor of Mortality Risk than Sleep Duration: A Prospective Cohort Study." *Sleep* 47, no. 1 (January 2024): zsad253. https://doi.org/10.1093/sleep/zsad253.

World Health Organization. "Deafness and Hearing Loss: Safe Listening." Updated February 23, 2022. https://www.who.int/news-room/questions-and-answers/item /deafness-and-hearing-loss-safe-listening.

Mind

Ballard, Parissa J., Lindsay T. Hoyt, and Mark C. Pachucki. "Impacts of Adolescent and Young Adult Civic Engagement on Health and Socioeconomic Status in Adulthood." *Child Development* 90, no. 4 (2018): 1138–1154. https://doi.org/10.1111/cdev.12998.

Cialdini, Robert B., and Melanie R. Trost. "Social Influence: Social Norms, Conformity and Compliance." In *The Handbook of Social Psychology,* edited by Daniel T. Gilbert, Susan T. Fiske, and Gardner Lindzey, 151–192. New York: McGraw-Hill, 1998.

Cousins, James N., Kian F. Wong, Bindiya L. Raghunath, Carol Look, and Michael W. L. Chee. "The Long-Term Memory Benefits of a Daytime Nap Compared with Cramming." *Sleep* 42, no. 1 (2018): zsy207. https://doi.org/10.1093/sleep/zsy207.

Gollwitzer, Peter M. "Implementation Intentions: Strong Effects of Simple Plans." *American Psychologist* 54, no. 7 (1999): 493–503. https://doi.org/10.1037/0003-066x.54.7.493.

Han, Ke-Tsung, and Li-Wen Ruan. "Effects of Indoor Plants on Self-Reported Perceptions: A Systemic Review." *Sustainability* 11, no. 16 (2019): 4506. https://doi.org/10.3390/su11164506.

Kraft, Tara L., and Sarah D. Pressman. "Grin and Bear It." *Psychological Science* 23, no. 11 (2012): 1372–78. https://doi.org/10.1177/0956797612445312.

Lally, Phillippa, Cornelia H. M. van Jaarsveld, Henry W. W. Potts, and Jane Wardle. "How Are Habits Formed: Modelling Habit Formation in the Real World." *European Journal of Social Psychology* 40, no. 6 (2010): 998–1009. https://doi.org/10.1002/ejsp.674.

Lee, Min-sun, Juyoung Lee, Bum-Jin Park, and Yoshifumi Miyazaki. "Interaction with Indoor Plants May Reduce Psychological and Physiological Stress by Suppressing Autonomic Nervous System Activity in Young Adults: A Randomized Crossover Study." *Journal of Physiological Anthropology* 34, no. 1 (2015). https://doi.org/10.1186/s40101-015-0060-8.

Mårtensson, Johan, Johan Eriksson, Nils Christian Bodammer, Magnus Lindgren, Mikael Johansson, Lars Nyberg, and Martin Lövdén. "Growth of Language-Related Brain Areas after Foreign Language Learning." *NeuroImage* 63, no. 1 (2012): 240–44. https://doi.org/10.1016/j.neuroimage.2012.06.043.

Nakao, Mutsuhiro. "Special Series on 'Effects of Board Games on Health Education and Promotion' Board Games as a Promising Tool for Health Promotion: A Review of Recent Literature." *BioPsychoSocial Medicine* 13, no. 1 (2019). https://doi.org/10.1186/s13030-019-0146-3.

Olulade, O. A., Nasheed I. Jamal, Daniel S. Koo, Charles A. Perfetti, Carol LaSasso, and Guinevere F. Eden. "Neuroanatomical Evidence in Support of the Bilingual Advantage Theory." *Cerebral Cortex* 26, no. 7 (2015): 3196–3204. https://doi.org/10.1093/cercor/bhv152.

Park, Guihyun, Beng-Chong Lim, and Hui Si Oh. "Why Being Bored Might Not Be a Bad Thing after All." *Academy of Management Discoveries* 5, no. 1 (2019): 78–92. https://doi.org/10.5465/amd.2017.0033.

Pressman, Sarah D., Amanda M. Acevedo, Katherine V. Hammond, and Tara L. Kraft-Feil. "Smile (or Grimace) through the Pain? The Effects of Experimentally Manipulated Facial Expressions on Needle-Injection Responses." *Emotion* 21, no. 6 (2021): 1188–1203. https://doi.org/10.1037/emo0000913.

Roster, Catherine A., Joseph R. Ferrari, and M. Peter Jurkat. "The Dark Side of Home: Assessing Possession 'Clutter' on Subjective Well-Being." *Journal of Environmental Psychology* 46 (June 2016): 32–41. https://doi.org/10.1016/j.jenvp.2016.03.003.

Tedeschi, Tim. "Regular Blueberry Consumption May Reduce Risk of Dementia, Study Finds." UC News. May 10, 2022. https://www.uc.edu/news/articles/2022/05/blueberries-may-lower-chances-of-dementia-research-finds.html.

Spirit

Adams, Gabrielle S., Francis J. Flynn, and Michael I. Norton. "The Gifts We Keep on Giving." *Psychological Science* 23, no. 10 (2012): 1145–50. https://doi.org/10.1177/0956797612439718.

Bennett, Mary Payne, and Cecile Lengacher. "Humor and Laughter May Influence Health IV. Humor and Immune Function." *Evidence-Based Complementary and Alternative Medicine* 6, no. 2 (2009): 159–64. https://doi.org/10.1093/ecam/nem149.

Bloom, Jessica de, Sabine A. E. Geurts, and Michiel A. J. Kompier. "Vacation (After-) Effects on Employee Health and Well-Being, and the Role of Vacation Activities, Experiences and Sleep." *Journal of Happiness Studies* 14, no. 2 (2012): 613–33. https://doi.org/10.1007/s10902-012-9345-3.

Brotons, Melissa, Susan M. Koger, and Patty Pickett-Cooper. "Music and Dementias: A Review of Literature." *Journal of Music Therapy* 34, no. 4 (1997): 204–45. https://doi.org/10.1093/jmt/34.4.204.

Centers for Disease Control and Prevention. "How to Stay Healthy around Pets and Other Animals." Updated May 5, 2023. https://www.cdc.gov/healthypets/keeping-pets-and-people-healthy/how.html.

Chen, Yu, Gloria Mark, and Sanna Ali. "Promoting Positive Affect through Smartphone Photography." *Psychology of Well-Being* 6, no. 1 (2016). https://doi.org/10.1186/s13612-016-0044-4.

Chikani, Vatsal, Douglas Reding, Paul Gunderson, and Catherine A. McCarty. "Vacations Improve Mental Health among Rural Women: The Wisconsin Rural Women's Health Study." *WMJ: Official Publication of the State Medical Society of Wisconsin* 104, no. 6 (2005): 20–23. https://pubmed.ncbi.nlm.nih.gov/16218311/.

Collins, Hanne K., Serena F. Hagerty, Jordi Quoidbach, Michael I. Norton, and Alison Wood Brooks. "Relational Diversity in Social Portfolios Predicts Well-Being." *Proceedings of the National Academy of Sciences* 119, no. 43 (2022). https://doi.org/10.1073/pnas.2120668119.

Dueren, Anna L., Aikaterini Vafeiadou, Christopher Edgar, and Michael J. Banissy. "The Influence of Duration, Arm Crossing Style, Gender, and Emotional Closeness on Hugging Behaviour." *Acta Psychologica* 221 (November 2021): 103441. https://doi.org/10.1016/j.actpsy.2021.103441.

Emmons, Robert A., and Michael E. McCullough. "Counting Blessings versus Burdens: An Experimental Investigation of Gratitude and Subjective Well-Being in Daily Life." *Journal of Personality & Social Psychology* 84, no. 2 (2003): 377–89. https://doi.org/10.1037//0022 -3514.84.2.377.

Falk, John H., Nicole Claudio, David Meier, and Judith Koke. "Measuring the Public & Economic Value of Art Museum Experiences." Institute for Learning Innovation. March 3, 2023. https://www.instituteforlearninginnovation.org/wp-content/uploads/2022/11/FINAL -Measuring-the-Public-Value-of-Art-Museums-TECHNICAL-REPORT2.1.pdf.

Fancourt, Daisy, Saoirse Finn, Katey Warran, and Theresa Wiseman. "Group Singing in Bereavement: Effects on Mental Health, Self-Efficacy, Self-Esteem and Well-Being." *BMJ Supportive & Palliative Care* 12, (2019): e607–e615. https://doi.org/10.1136/bmjspcare -2018-001642.

Feltz, Deborah L., Norbert L. Kerr, and Brandon C. Irwin. "Buddy Up: The Köhler Effect Applied to Health Games." *Journal of Sport and Exercise Psychology* 33, no. 4 (2011): 506–26. https://doi.org/10.1123/jsep.33.4.506.

Giles, Lynne C., Gary F. V. Glonek, Mary A. Luszcz, and Gary R. Andrews. "Effect of Social Networks on 10 Year Survival in Very Old Australians: The Australian Longitudinal Study of Aging." *Journal of Epidemiology & Community Health* 59, no. 7 (2005): 574–79. https:// doi.org/10.1136/jech.2004.025429.

Greater Good in Action. "Random Acts of Kindness." University of California, Berkeley. 2018. https://ggia.berkeley.edu/practice/practice_as_pdf/random_acts_of_kindness.

Gump, Brooks B., and Karen A. Matthews. "Are Vacations Good for Your Health? The 9-Year Mortality Experience after the Multiple Risk Factor Intervention Trial." *Psychosomatic Medicine* 62, no. 5 (2000): 608–12. https://doi.org/10.1097/00006842-200009000 -00003.

Hawkley, Louise C., and John T. Cacioppo. "Loneliness Matters: A Theoretical and Empirical Review of Consequences and Mechanisms." *Annals of Behavioral Medicine* 40, no. 2 (2010): 218–27. https://www.ncbi.nlm.nih.gov/pmc/articles/PMC3874845/.

Heller, Aaron S., Tracey C. Shi, C. E. Chiemeka Ezie, Travis R. Reneau, Lara M. Baez, Conor J. Gibbons, and Catherine A. Hartley. "Association between Real-World Experiential Diversity and Positive Affect Relates to Hippocampal–Striatal Functional Connectivity." *Nature Neuroscience* 23, no. 7 (2020): 800–804. https://doi.org/10.1038/s41593-020-0636-4.